We Share the Name Refugee

A MILLION STEPS OF FAITH

THE FOUNDRY
PUBLISHING

We Share the Name Refugee

A MILLION STEPS OF FAITH

Editor
Mike L. Wonch
Director of Editorial
Bonnie Perry
Writer
Teanna Sunberg

Photo credits:
Chris Khoury: pp. 32, 58
Nazarene Compassionate Ministries/Jon Morton: pp. 6, 14, 22, 40
Nazarene Compassionate Ministries/Brandon Sipes: p. 48

Beacon Hill Press of Kansas City
PO Box 419527
Kansas City, MO 64141
nph.com

ISBN: 978-0-8341-3664-9

Printed in the
United States of America

10 9 8 7 6 5 4 3 2 1

CONTENTS

Introduction

Dear Reader,

I fear that what you search for in these pages, you will not find. This is neither a comprehensive nor a fair account of the hardships and heartbreak experienced by more than a million people who made, and continue to make, their journey into Europe. Because this author has not experienced the trauma of fleeing war, nor the terror of the sea, nor the obstacle of closed borders, her work is flawed. In fact, this author crossed easily over borders and slept comfortably in beds in heated rooms while the people described in these pages slept in tents and shivered through the night. Thus, this is neither a fair account nor a fair world.

Every person you meet within these pages tells their story with as much accuracy as the author could produce. Every person, except one . . . Eden. She is either the only fictional character in these pages or the most authentic. You see, Eden is us. Eden is the voice of our Facebook posts and the conversations we whisper when we think no one is listening. Eden says what we think and what we're afraid to say. Eden gives voice to our fears and to our prejudices. Eden is you. Eden is me.

As you read, please remember that our creation story begins in a garden called Eden, and that we each trace our identity back to Genesis—the beginning. It is the place where we once dwelled in perfect union with our Creator and with each other, and it is the place where we lost ourselves in sin. It is from there that we discover we are on a journey—in exile, if you will. You see, *we share the name refugee* with each other, and with a God who left His home and began His life in exile in Egypt for us (Matthew 2:13-15).

As we travel through these stories, I wish you courage for the journey, because finding our way home is an honest search and *a million steps of faith.*

With courage,

Eden Walker

Teanna Sunberg (writer) is a justice advocate for refugees and anti-trafficking, and lectures on missiology and intercultural studies. A published author and an ordained elder in the Church of the Nazarene, she serves the Central Europe Field from Budapest, Hungary. She and her husband Jay have ministered in Russia, Bulgaria and Hungary. They have four daughters. Find her blog at "http://centraleuropenaz.org."

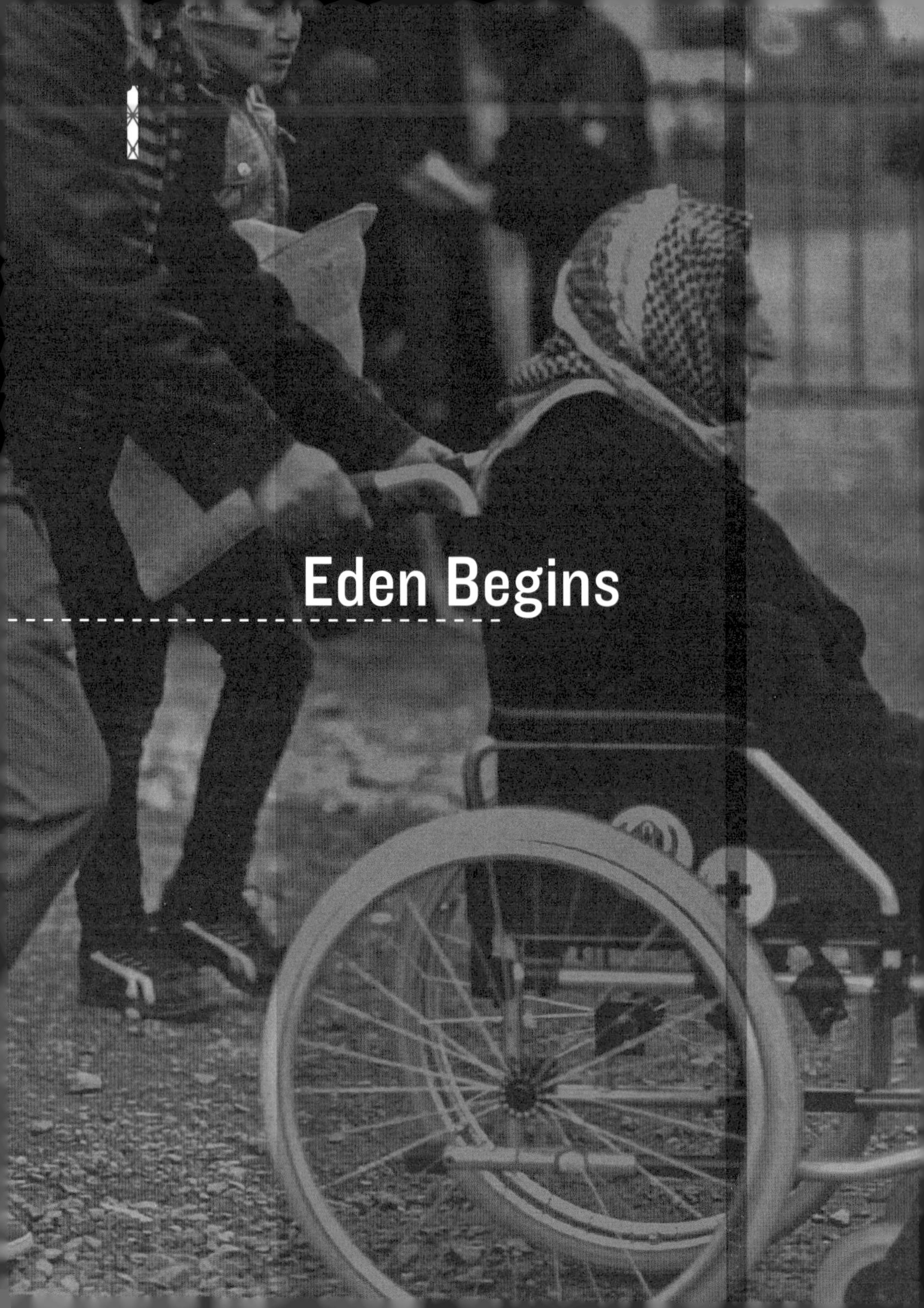

1

Eden Begins

Late summer 2015, at the EKO gas station in Northern Greece

I sat at a table in the gas station and watched them. Across the highway, a sea of people seemed to be in endless motion. They were Middle Eastern, as evidenced by the women covered in hijabs[1] and robes. I watched them and wondered: *Who were they? What brought them? Were there terrorists among them?* Sure, I knew how that sounded—it sounded racist. But it was honest—honest fear. I read the papers. I watched the news. I was paid to *report* the news, for that matter. These people were Muslims, and that meant something.

Taking a sip of my soda, I played with the euro coin in my hand. *Am I racist?* I considered the question as I squinted across the highway. Cautious, yes. But racist? No. I had a responsibility to be cautious, to protect myself and my family from danger.

My gyro sandwich lay open beside me. Tasty, with its roasted meat and fresh greens, but who had prepared it? Had they washed their hands? People had different understandings of cleanliness, especially in foreign places. I flicked a napkin over the top to hide how much would be wasted. The woman behind the counter laid a tiny piece of paper on the table. The writing was barely legible and in Greek—so, not readable at all. Were they charging too much?

A movement across the highway drew my eye back to the window. I could feel the distance of our two worlds—mine and theirs. Non-Muslim and Muslim. White and brown. Safe and savage. I shifted, unsure of where that last thought had come from, and embarrassed I had even thought it.

Wealthy and poor. But were they poor? The Saudis were rich, but the Syrians? The Afghanis were poor. But they were refugees, so they must be poor. Right? Refugees were poor—everybody knew that, didn't they? I pushed the

1. A veil or headscarf traditionally worn by Muslim women to symbolize privacy and modesty.

annoying questions aside, stood up, and braced myself to get the job done. *Get the photos and get out, Eden*, I told myself. The only thing that lay between me and the safety of my hotel room was this simple job. I was in Greece to cover a different story, but having stumbled on this camp that seemed to have popped up overnight, I was hoping that a few freelance photos might earn me some extra cash. I checked to ensure my passport and credit cards still lay securely under my shirt where nobody could take them. Lost documents meant no way out of this country. No documents meant no travel—and being trapped here was a frightening prospect. I shuddered and muttered, "Just get the job done, Eden."

Photos for Sale

My discovery of refugees at the EKO gas station would lead me on a journey crisscrossing the Balkan Peninsula, and it bolstered what had been a mediocre freelance income. Northern Greece and that gas station were about to explode—however, as I crossed the highway that summer, these places had yet to attract the international media's map of interest. Yes, Middle Eastern refugees were already using the EKO gas station as a stop before the border with the former Yugoslav Republic of Macedonia, but at that time, it was still a sleepy little place—a place completely unprepared for the storm that was coming.

By September, the world was glued to their newsfeeds as the Balkan Highway route became a conduit for a human tidal wave. Hungary, with its thousands of refugees amassed in Budapest's Keleti station, was my next stop. I wanted to be there to cover what might be the beginning of a coordinated jihad in Europe.

Looking back, I suppose that Bara'ah and her baby Zinat were somewhere in Greece, probably up by Lesvos, as I made that first journey across the highway. While Bara'ah traveled with a nursing baby in her arms, moved past the Greek border, traversed two more countries, and made the heart-sinking discovery that they had missed the Hungarian border closure by a mere 24 hours, I sold those first freelance photos from the EKO station and celebrated my good fortune. Not only had the photos been much easier to sell than I'd anticipated, they had opened up opportunities for more freelance jobs.

It was October when I met Bara'ah at the border between Croatia and Slovenia, and that brief encounter began to pull at the fraying edges of my tightly woven ideas about Middle Eastern people and the wave of asylum-seekers they became. Maybe I recognized that while we were both women whose journeys had run geographically parallell, her experience as an undocumented Muslim woman fleeing Afghanistan was much different than mine. Either way, I was impacted by the realization that Bara'ah had courageously crossed over countries and the very real dangers that awaited her while carrying two weights—baby Zinat on her hip, and an ache in her heart for the husband she had left behind in Kabul.

I came to understand that just as Greece was the beginning of my story, it was the beginning of the European chapter of Bara'ah's story. Like so many other refugees, Bara'ah found the vast, unpredictable Mediterranean and the often-violent land of Bulgaria to be the bridge (the touchstones) of her long journey. I had yet to realize how the story of one refugee mother, along with the stories of 1.5 million others entering Europe, would create a narrative of fear in me.

In late summer 2015, at the invitation of Germany's chancellor, they came from their homes in Syria, Afghanistan, Iraq, Pakistan, as well as the even more-distant North African countries, and began to crash upon European shores with unprecedented power. These thousands of stories intersected with

Europe across the highway from where I sat, and as they did, they shot a spear of fear into my heart. I felt we were being invaded.

For Bara'ah and baby Zinat, Idomeni's teeming pot of 15,000 stranded inhabitants did not yet exist. They were simply part of the first wave—a Muslim mother carrying her baby to safety, one painful step at a time. How the media saw her, how Europe received her, and how the so-called Christian West responded to her depended so much on the story that was told[2] and the reporter who told it. That reporter was me. I am Eden.

A Mother and Baby Begin their Journey

Bara'ah shifted the baby on her hip and wiggled her toes. They ached.[3] Her red tennis shoes were a bit too small—just enough so that each time she took a step, her toes strained for freedom against the canvas. Somewhere after Lesvos, after the sea, someone had given her these shoes. Could she have asked them for a larger size? She hardly remembered how she had received the clothes she now wore. But the journey across the sea—cold, wet rags clinging to her body, the swell of the crashing waves—those were sensations she would never forget.

Zinat whimpered in her arms. Bara'ah adjusted her pink cap and kissed her cheek. Boarding that boat in Turkey, she could never have imagined how the waves would threaten to tear her baby from her arms, how each crash would slap at her breath, or how hard it would be to simply survive. ●

2. News from October 16, 2016. <http://www.balkaninsight.com/en/article/slovenian-migrant
-border-fence-could-lead-to-violence-10-24-2016>

3. I met her in October at the border between Croatia and Slovenia or Slovakia. Many helped translate. She probably came through Lesvos/Greece in September.

Reflect on this . . .

What images come to mind when you hear the word "refugee"?

What emotions do you experience when you see refugees in the media?

Do you think what you believe about refugees is accurate or valid?

NOTES:

NOTES:

2

Eden Closes

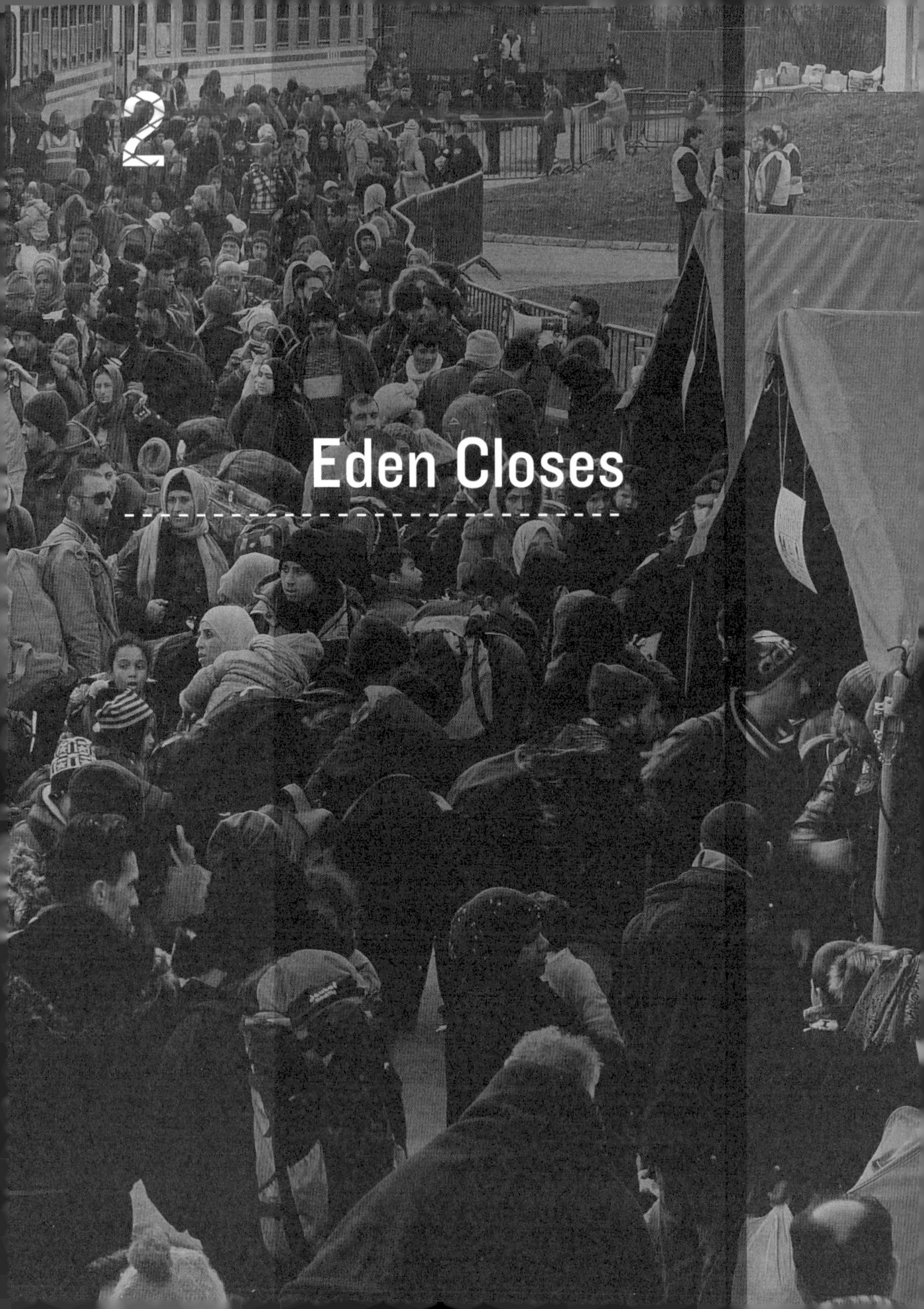

September 2015, at Keleti train station in Budapest, Hungary

As I arrived at the Keleti train station that morning, I was unprepared for what I found. The once organized and stately train station in the center of Hungary's capitol had been transformed into something foreign. The "other" was everywhere I looked—and she wore a hijab and was thousands strong. I was speechless. *No wonder the media is in a frenzy,* I thought.

Covering my nose as I walked by the stench of the six temporary toilets that had been placed at the end of the plaza, I began to snap photos of the chaos. One of the toilets was already oozing liquid onto the pavement. People were everywhere—however, unlike the constant motion of people on a big city street, this was humanity going nowhere. Clothes and shoes hung on any available outcropping—blankets, tents and people were everywhere. The crowds were applying increasing pressure to the surrounding area. Would the human wave continue to amass and eventually crest the wall? Or would the dam—the Hungarian government—begin to break and allow a way through?

For a journalist, timing is key. I was there partly because, with so many Arabs in one place, representing different religious factions of Islam—Sunni, Shias, and Allowei—I expected a riot at any time. The crowd also included ethnicities that had inner-Arab tensions—Iraqis, Kurds, Kurdish Christians, Yazidis, Afghanis, and Pakistanis. Added to that were Europe's political extremists. With Hungary refusing to let any asylum-seekers board trains to Austria—or anywhere else in the European Union[4] for that matter—people could not move forward, and nobody was willing to turn back. It was a stalemate.

4. The European Union (EU) is a political and economic union of 28 member states that are located primarily in Europe. It has an area of 4,475,757 km, and an estimated population of over 510 million. <https://en.wikipedia.org/wiki/European_Union.> Accessed March 28, 2017.

While I waited, I gathered stories. My goal was to photograph groups of military-aged young men. In photographs they appeared intimidating, like an invading army dressed in jeans and hoodies. People in the West were talking about a "Trojan Horse," and that was a good storyline for me. It played well on fear, an emotion I found to be quite powerful and easy to manipulate. Looking around, I saw a newsstand to my left and purchased the day's edition of the French newspaper.

The Newlyweds

Hiba watched the foreign woman walking among the blankets. Their corner spot on the floor, just inside the train station, was a prime space with a roof and shops nearby. There was even a small wall to lean on. Last night, when they had first arrived, Muhammad had laid down a blanket and had fallen asleep almost immediately, tired after the long journey. With her sister Aisha on one side and Muhammad on the other, she had stayed somewhat warm, but now she shivered in the morning mist. The woman wandered back and forth. She seemed to be looking for somebody. A camera swung at her side, and she was dressed in Western clothes. Hungarian? British? American? It was hard to tell. As the woman drew closer, Hiba lowered her eyes.

Suddenly, the woman was before her, snapping a photo. The woman was speaking, but Hiba struggled to keep up and string the English syllables into meaning.

"Can I interview you?" the woman asked, kneeling down.

She was neither young nor old, Hiba observed. Younger than her own mother in Aleppo? Yes. But without a hijab, it was difficult to tell her age. Why would this stranger want to speak with her? She shrugged, hesitant to use her

English. "Yes?" The word slipped from her lips. She worried that it was too heavily accented to be intelligible.

At her response, the woman laid yesterday's newspaper on the floor and prepared to sit on top of it. Hiba recognized the front-page photo, which was of the people in the opposite corner of the train station. Hiba stopped her and pulled a nicer cover from her bag. She laid the cover down and invited the woman to sit on it.

"My name is Eden," the woman said. She spoke easily and simply. "I want to hear your story. Where are you from?"

"I . . . we," she glanced at Muhammad, "are from Homs." Hiba licked her lips and returned the woman's smile. She could feel Muhammad watching now, as her sister returned the woman's brown-eyed gaze.

"Homs?" The woman wrote something quickly in her notebook. "Can I ask you why you left there?"

"Surely you know. Surely you have heard about the war in Syria?" Mohammad leaned in now, his eyes intense, his voice incredulous.

Hiba watched the woman's reaction. Obviously she knew, so why the question?

"Yes." There was the smile again. "Yes, I know what I read in the newspapers, but I want to hear your story. Why did you leave?" Hiba watched Muhammad settle in to respond and felt pride surge in her breast. He was handsome, and his English was good. He would speak for her and her sister.

"There is a war," Muhammad said wearily. "There is danger—too much danger. I took my wife and her sister and we left," There was kindness in his face.

"Yes, I know a little about the war. She is your wife?" The woman nodded at Hiba. Muhammad looked at her with a smile in his brown eyes. "Yes, she is my wife." He said it with pride.

"And her sister is your wife, too?" The woman's eyebrows rose in a question.

"No," said Muhammad, laughing. "Just one wife. She is enough for me."

"How long have you been traveling?" The woman went back to the story.

"Well," said Muhammad, pausing to count, "we have been married 28 days, and we left three days after the wedding, so, 25 days."

The woman's eyes widened. "You're newly married?"

Hiba wanted to speak. "Yes, he is my husband now."

"So why? How?" The woman seemed to be at a loss. "Why did you leave?"

Sighing, Muhammad said, "It was not an easy decision. The national forces came to my door, told me I had to report for military duty in two days. But, for which side should I fight? I have friends fighting on both sides. I don't want to kill anybody and I don't want to get killed. So, I took my wife and her sister, and we fled in the night. I hope we can make a home somewhere. I was studying to be an engineer. I want to work. I just want to live in peace."

September 15, 2015, on the Röske railroad tracks—Serbian side of the border with Hungary

Zinat wanted to nurse, but Bara'ah pushed on. She had no choice—she didn't know how much longer she could keep going. If she missed the border closure . . . she shuddered to think. Hearing a sharp gasp behind her, she turned without thinking. A pregnant girl had stopped, doubled over. Her young husband stood by her side. "My water." She looked up at Bara'ah with panicked eyes. "My waters have broken. The baby is coming."

Bara'ah looked at the young husband. In another situation, she would not have interfered, but today was different. "Can you carry her? You must carry her. The border is very close. Give me your bag and I will help you." Reaching down, she added the heavy bag to her shoulder, where her own bag already dangled. With Zinat on her hip, she set her eyes on the railroad tracks. "One step at a time. Just one step at a time." Bara'ah knew that on the Hungarian side, there would be doctors.

"The border is close," she heard somebody say. "Maybe five more minutes. Maybe 10."

I can do 10 more minutes, she said to herself.

Pausing, Bara'ah laid a hand on the woman's shoulder. "You must breathe, slow and steady, even when the pains come. Listen to me. There are doctors on the other side and they will help you birth this baby, but you must keep going. This baby must wait until we cross the border." The young woman wiped a tear from her cheek and nodded as Bara'ah turned and continued on.

Words began to ripple through the crowd. "Closed. They have closed the border early." Bara'ah clutched Zinat closer and felt her heart begin to beat in her ears.

"What?" She cried to the old man walking next to her. "What did they say?"

He quickened his pace, barely looking her way. "Closed."

As they drew closer, she saw reporters on the Serbian side of the fence talking into big cameras and microphones. Behind them, there was no longer any opening to pass through. Hungarian police and military in riot gear reinforced the fence.

Dropping her heavy bags to the ground, Bara'ah would have run to the fence to see with her own eyes if there was any small way to squeeze through. Maybe the guards would let a mother and baby pass. But the sharp cry behind her swung her around.

"The baby is coming," cried the young father. "The baby is coming now!"

Reflect on this . . .

What is the last stressful situation you faced?

In what ways did this situation impact your life?

In what ways can we reach out to those who are facing a stressful situation in our community or somewhere around the world?

NOTES:

3

Eden Remembers

September 18, 2015, at the border between Croatia and Slovenia

When the Hungarian government closed the Röszke border earlier than expected, the tide of people redirected within hours. Coordinates that turned the human migration toward Croatia and on to Slovenia were relayed through Facebook and WhatsApp. The diversion added two days by foot to the trip, but the way into the EU was open.

Having photographed the people trapped in "no man's land" on the railroad tracks, I moved toward the next stalemate—the border point between Croatia and Slovenia. By the time I reached it, nearly 2,000 people had pooled at the checkpoint, waiting before a wall of Croatian police outfitted in riot gear. Water cannons and tear gas had been deployed against those denied entry at Röszke, so I was unsure what to expect now. Still, the crowds of travelers, as usual, seemed calm yet determined. As for me, my only purpose there was to gather more photos.

Shoes

Bara'ah stepped down from the bus and shifted Zinat's weight in her arms. Her heart was heavier than the baby, heavier than the bag, heavier than the dreams she carried and the pain of the last two months. She wondered about her husband back in Kabul. She thought of him selling cigarettes at the little corner store and wondered if he would ever get to see his baby again.

Falling into step with others from the bus, she followed the crowd toward the bridge where border signs announced entry into Slovenia. Uniformed guards in riot gear blocked the way. She noted the medical van parked on the road and the mouth-watering smell of hot food. She could see a woman in a tent bent over an outdoor stove, stirring a huge vat of liquid. Her stomach rumbled. It had been days since she had eaten real food—since before Röszke.

She pushed the thought away. Unconsciously, she rubbed a spot on her arm where she had been hit by a water cannon. She still couldn't believe the border guards had used tear gas—she had feared for Zinat's lungs and eyes.

Coming as close to the border with Slovenia as was allowed, Bara'ah finally set down the heavy bag, then spread out a small blanket for the baby. Laying the sleeping bundle down, she relished the freedom of empty arms, even though they ached. She hoped they could make it to Germany before the weather turned colder.

When Zinat woke, Bara'ah gathered her things and made her way to the clothes tent. She hoped for different shoes that would fit her. Every step was agony. The line moved quickly, and suddenly she found herself being addressed in Arabic. The accent was Egyptian and the woman smiled gently. Bara'ah gave her size and waited, looking around until she spotted a woman with a camera. She was familiar. Where had she seen her? Then she remembered—the woman had been at the border, one of the photographers snapping photos as the young mother gave birth with only the trees to protect her from strangers' eyes. Maybe she knew something about the new mother and the baby. Were they okay? She returned her attention back to the Egyptian woman and asked her quietly if she could translate into English.

"Hello?" she spoke now through Hany, the Egyptian woman. The reporter looked around, surprised. "I am Bara'ah. This is my baby, Zinat. I saw you at Röszke."

The reporter responded, "Yes, I remember you. You were there at the birth of that baby on the border." She took a step toward Bara'ah. "Do you know what happened to the mother and baby?"

Bara'ah's smiled slipped. "No . . . I was hoping you knew."

"Me? No, I moved on to take more photos. So, you finally made it here. How did you come?"

"I walked some," said Bara'ah, holding up the shoes Hany had given her. "And there was a bus part of the way too."

The woman nodded. "My name is Eden," she said, glancing down at the baby in Bara'ah's arms. "Is your husband here?"

Bara'ah's smile wilted again and she sighed. "No. My husband is still in Kabul."

"Why?" Eden asked.

"We did not have enough money for all of us. The smuggler charges us half-price for the baby, but still, my husband makes a very small salary at the cigarette stand. My family gave some money so I could take the baby, but he is . . . he is still there."

Eden shrugged. "So he'll come later, then?"

Bara'ah looked down at her baby. "Maybe. I hope. But—"

"Oh, sorry," Eden interrupted. "I need to get this photo. It was nice meeting you. Maybe I'll see you again?"

Bara'ah watched Eden rush away, glanced down at the shoes that dangled from her fingers, and wandered back to the hill. She laid out her blanket again, laid Zinat down, and waited (two nights, sleeping in the open air without a tent to cover them) for the border with Slovenia to open.

October 2015, at Bobska transit point between Serbian and Croatia

I looked up into the October sky and shivered as the cold bit through my overcoat and thermal shell, seeping deep into my bones. *Could it be any colder?* I thought irritably. Getting paid to track down stories had its cost.

Readers responded to any article about Middle Easterners' plans to infiltrate the West. Audiences feed on fear, and that fear sold the stories I was getting paid to write. The more fear I stoked in my readers, the more money I made. But the longer I interviewed people working in grassroots refugee response, the harder it was to find sources to support that angle.

I was hopeful that a lead from the Czech Republic, a woman named Tereza, would be a good source for a story portraying the refugees' violent nature. To their credit, the Czech government had come down hard on closing borders and rejected their EU quota of 1,500 asylum-seekers. They'd retained their sovereignty, stating that they would only take 600 refugees, all of which must be from a Christian background. Muslim refugees were not welcome.

I'd been directed to an unofficial border crossing between Serbia and Croatia called Bobska and told to look for a tall, blond woman in a Czech Team jacket. My eyes scanned for Tereza amongst the people waiting in the mud. *There must be at least 2,000 of them.* I shook my head. Then I spotted Tereza's white-blonde hair bobbing alongside a border guard. I moved toward her until I saw the guard waving a baton at the wave of people pressing against the gate.

Tereza held a child, maybe five years old, and seemed to be negotiating with a frantic mother on the other side of the fence. I couldn't hear what she said, but Tereza's features were animated as she turned and spoke to the angry guard. He responded with shouts as the mother and child wailed. They were so close that they could almost touch, had it not been for the cattle gate and guard separating them.

"Hi, I'm Eden." I took a step toward Tereza and the child. "This is quite a mess, isn't it?"

Tereza looked up at me and grimaced. "That's one word for it. Inhumane is what it is." She made a sweeping gesture above the mass of heads—women in their headscarves and trench coats, men with their black eyes and unshaven olive skin.

"I'm a reporter and photographer, freelance. Can I interview you while you're sitting here?"

Tereza motioned to the space next to the child. "Be my guest."

"What's happening here at Bobska?" I asked as I dropped down beside her. "Explain it to me."

She sighed and went silent for a few seconds. "Well, what you see here at Bobska, this is the 21st-century glimpse into Rachel's mourning for her children. It's a reference to an Old Testament mother who weeps for her dead child."

"I'm familiar with the story." I picked at a wilted piece of grass, unsure where she was going with this.

"When Rachel's fear becomes a reality, it's that utter desolation that comes when hope dies. Look around. What you see here is hope gasping for its last breath." She motioned to the mother behind the fence who still cried for her daughter. "And that sound that slices through your heart? That's Rachel weeping for her children."

"What happens when they turn violent?" I nodded toward the crowds. "How are you going to protect yourself?" I motioned to the great wall of people facing the border guards in their riot gear.

Tereza smiled grimly. "I've been here for weeks. I haven't seen them turn violent yet, even when they're beaten."

"There was Röszke at the Hungarian border," I retorted. "They rioted, remember?"

"Yes, there was Röszke. They closed the border seven hours earlier than the deadline.

"Families had been walking nonstop for days to make it in time." She shook her head sadly. "It was . . . tragic." The word hung in the air between us for a moment. "Two thousand traumatized, exhausted, desperate people trapped between two borders like animals. I saw a baby delivered there, you know? Right on the border. And children with no food and very little water."

Suddenly, a shadow fell over us. "Miss? Tereza?" I looked up to see an Afghani man towering over us. He held a little boy by the hand.

"Yes, I am Tereza." She rose to her feet.

"Excuse me, Miss," he said in halting English, "but the boy's mother is sick." He gestured toward the child. Apologizing for his English, he continued. "She *fant*." At the look of confusion on Tereza's face, he tried again, stretching the vowel into two syllables. He waited, but Tereza's face registered no understanding. He mimed falling.

"Fainted! She fainted?" Tereza grasped his meaning.

"Yes, fainted." He repeated. "Her boy," he nodded toward the child again, "alone."

"So, who are you?" I broke in, immediately sensing a story. "You are family of this boy?"

Looking at me solemnly, he said, "My name Ahmed, but I am nobody. I see mother fall. Boy alone." He shrugged. "He is Afghani. And, I am Afghani. So, I picked him up . . . find doctor for mother. Somebody tell me to find

Tereza for help. I wait with the boy until mother is okay. No problem." He sat down on the hill, pulling the small child protectively to his chest, just as Tereza had done with the little girl.

With Ahmed's help, we put the pieces of the story together. A mother had been traveling with her eight-year-old daughter and three-year-old son. The swell of people had pushed them through the gates, and the eight-year-old's hand had slipped from her mother's. Exhausted, sick, and distraught as the crowd forced her toward the buses, leaving her daughter behind, the woman had fainted and was still unconscious. The daughter was stuck in the midst of several thousand strangers behind a border. And the son, who moments ago had been safely in his mother's arms, was alone and unprotected, save for the care of one Afghani stranger named Ahmed.

Reflect on this . . .

Think about a time when you needed help and an unlikely stranger came to your aid.

How we can we reach out to people in our community who need our help?

How we can we reach out to people around the world who need our help?

NOTES:

NOTES:

4

Eden Shivers

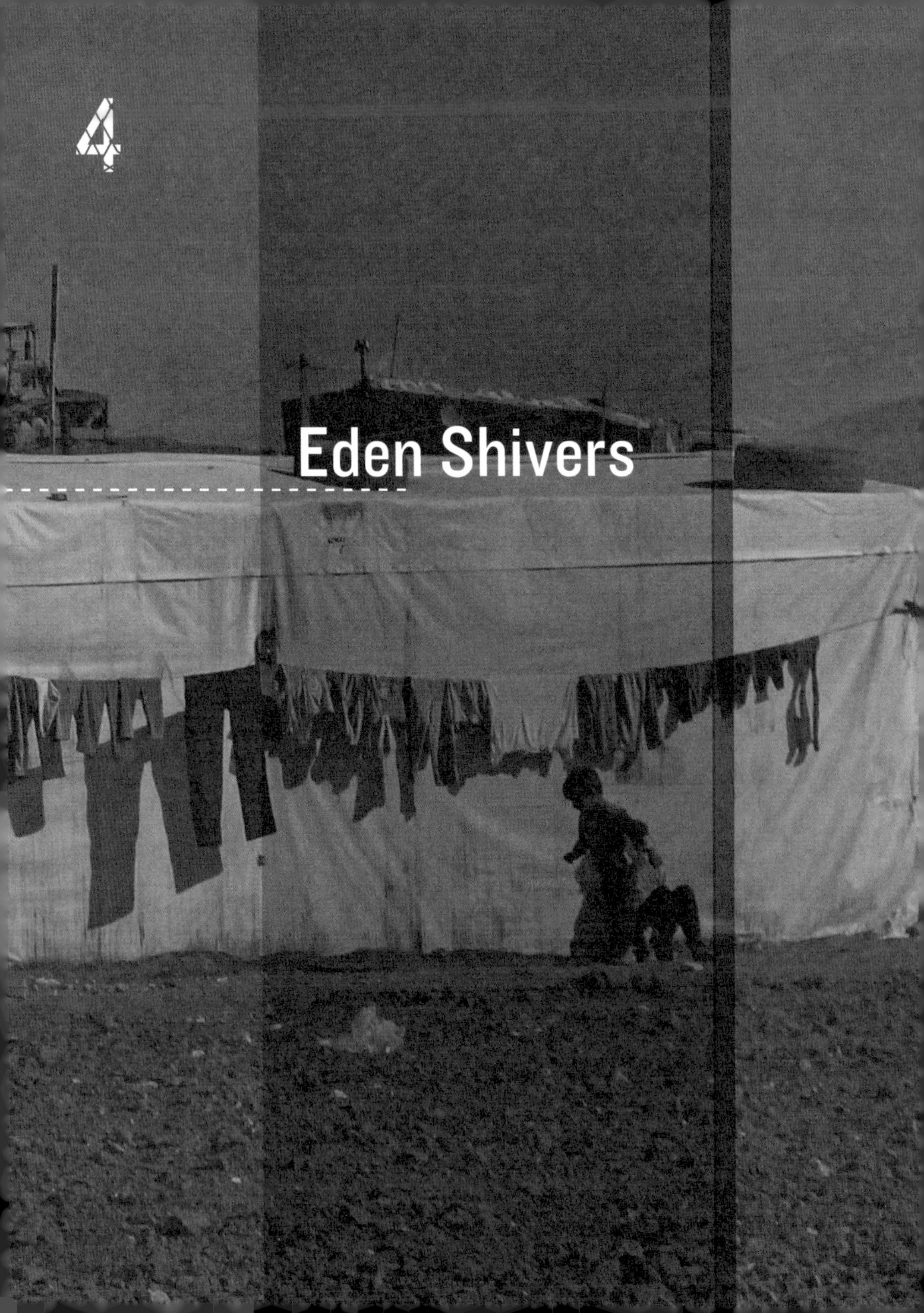

January 2016, at Slavonski Brod transit camp in Croatia

The January cold cut into my bones as the snow drove into my face, slowly dismantling my will to continue chasing this lead. I was struggling to feel my fingers, but my flimsy paper cup of hot chocolate was beginning to help.

As the railroad tracks behind me rumbled to life, my mind flashed pictures from my tour of the concentration camp in Auschwitz. The thought gave me a shiver that wasn't from the cold. Though I understood that this Croatian camp worked night and day to move people along on a northward journey, there was something eerily familiar about the train, the snow, the camp. The comparison was neither accurate nor fair, but it still rattled my nerves.

Somehow, I had been drawn into traveling across the Balkan Peninsula, fueled by the discovery that publishers were willing to pay me to follow the news as it broke. In the process, some mixed feelings were beginning to stir within me. I still believed these people posed a real danger, but at odd moments, I began to catch glimpses of the world through their eyes.

When those moments came, I tried to be objective. I reminded myself what I had already determined—that these people were part of an agenda, both political and ideological, that ultimately weakened the West. I stood with many others against the EU-imposed quota system, whereby every EU country would accept a certain number of refugees, and I maintained my opposition to the import of Middle Eastern religion and worldview. If people expected the West to open its doors, why wouldn't we expect their women could remove their head coverings? But of course, the problem went much deeper than hijabs. Their entire way of life pushed against our cultural sense of order, identity, and security.

My eyes shifted to the Croatian guard who stood at the end of the camp zone. Hundreds of people milled around the area, waiting for the guard to give them permission to move into the line to board the next train. It was a long, tedious wait in the freezing cold.

Hours earlier, while I stood in the clothes distribution tent seeking reprieve from the cold, an older man and a young boy had wheeled an elderly lady into the cavernous tent. It wasn't the first time I had seen a wheelchair on this journey, and once again, I marveled at the seeming impossibility of pushing a wheelchair through all manner of harsh terrain for days on end. I had also seen men with missing limbs navigate on crutches. But this time, the boy and his grandfather placed the shivering woman directly in front of a massive fan that heated the tent. As the woman turned her hijab-covered face toward the heat, she began to cry. It was not a shy, quiet flow of tears, but a raw, jagged weeping that shook me to my core.

Pushing the memory aside, I looked back to the guard. The black ski mask made his eyes the only clue to his humanity. I willed him to bark his commands at the crowd so I could snap my last photos and escape the frigid night. I knew he would divide the men and boys from the women and the children, then let the women and children go first to fill the train car. Afterward, he would allow the men and boys to squeeze into the standing space of the train. That was the photo I was after—one that showed only men standing in line. A photo like that spoke volumes.

A Story without Words

Maram watched the foreign lady sip the steaming hot chocolate. Her own children had just finished theirs—a warming treat in a paper cup as the snow drifted down. It would have been a charming scene if they weren't running from war, homeless, and hurtling toward a future they couldn't control. Still, the sweet, hot goodness of the chocolate had warmed their raw throats, and the heat from the cups had temporarily stilled their shivering. She looked down at her three children and felt a sense of pride in their strength. Her husband stood nearby, talking with a group of men they had met as they were being processed and fingerprinted. She hoped they had some news about what lay ahead in the journey.

This was a frightening step into an unknown future—they had encountered so many unanticipated roadblocks already. Maram had been surprised and confused by the fear she saw on the faces of the Europeans they met. Even the women refused to make eye contact with her. The bond between women, the bond of sisterhood and fellowship, was a pillar of her world. She missed her mother, her sisters, and her friends. *Will our family ever be together again?* she wondered. The answer was unclear, as was the rest of the future.

Drawing her mind away from the troubling thoughts, she glanced at the Croatian soldier who blocked their way forward. He was dressed in black, with a ski mask, gloves, boots, and coat covering everything except his dark eyes. He reminded her so much of . . . she shivered. The children had noticed too, remembered the black-clad groups of mercenaries that tore through Damascus in the last days before they fled. She needed to forget. The children needed to forget.

The foreign woman with the hot chocolate grabbed her attention again. At the same moment, the woman's eyes slipped to hers and they caught each other's gaze. Maram saw that there were questions between them. The foreigner did not look away.

"Mar-ha-ba." The woman stepped forward and spoke the greeting with a slight nod. The pronunciation was terrible, but Maram welcomed the distraction. Her 16-year-old daughter, Hasna, heard it too. Intrigued, the girl turned toward the foreigner.

"He-llo," Maram replied, trying the English sounds.

"Oh," the foreign woman exclaimed, "You speak English?"

Maram shook her head. "No. You speak Arabic?"

The foreign woman shook her head. There were questions in her eyes. "No. No Arabic." Her eyes jumped hopefully to Hasna. "English?"

"No English. Only Arabic," Maram said.

The snow fell, and the temperature seemed to drop even further as the two women stood in the glow of the hot chocolate kiosk. Each one had so much to say—so many stories to tell.

The guard suddenly shattered the stillness with an ear-splitting command. The message was clear to Maram—she was being ordered to move. To where and for what purpose, she had no idea. The destination, timing, and circumstances had long ago slipped from her control. She knew her time with this woman was ending. She needed to tell her story. She needed to leave a memory, a message that she had passed through this place, that she had existed and triumphed here in this moment of hot chocolate and snowflakes amid the raging storm. Turning as the line of women and children began to take shape, she took the woman's hands in her own.

"Damascus," Maram said earnestly. And with her hands fluttering upward, she mimicked the sound of a bomb, letting the pieces scatter in the night air and envelope them in a mushroom cloud.

The light reflected in the foreign woman's eyes wavered and flickered. Her smile faded, and she reached out and pulled Maram into an embrace. Then

Maram and her children got in line and continued their journey through the night. ●

Reflect on this . . .

When was the last time you had empathy for someone?

Why is it important to walk in someone else's shoes?

In what ways can we allow our compassion to grow for others?

NOTES:

NOTES:

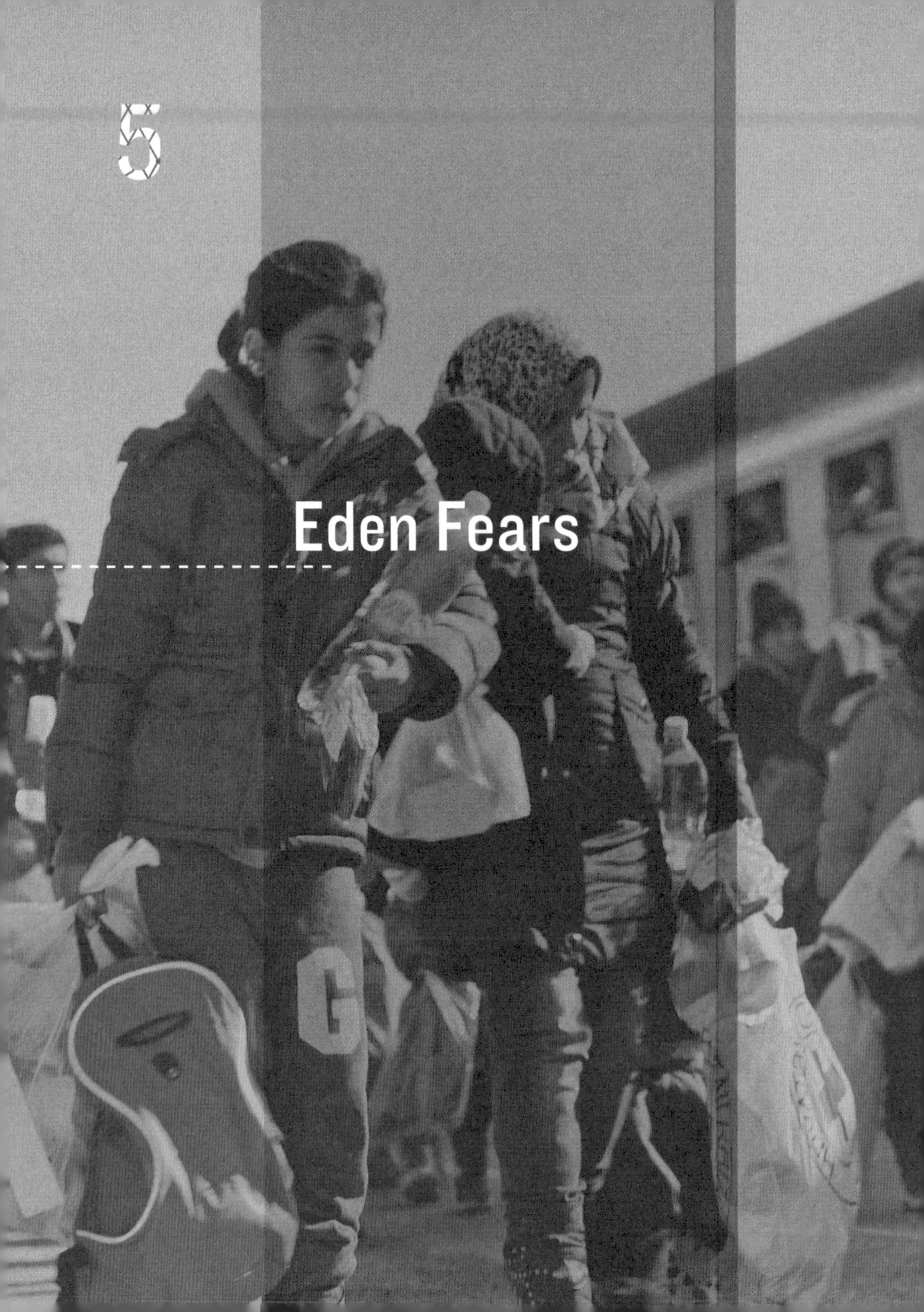

5

Eden Fears

March 2016, at EKO gas station

In the last several months, the EKO gas station had been transformed into a makeshift village for more than 1,500 refugees. Tents were everywhere, some with blue UNHCR[5] letters emblazoned across white canvas, others of the colorful camping variety. The air had a carnival feel, rich with the laughter of children and the buzz of voices. But then a bent, elderly woman in a hijab walked by, jolting me into reality: *They're dangerous and I'm surrounded.* The thought slipped out from the place deep inside where I kept those feelings hidden.

I had returned to Greece, this time on assignment with a pay-per-word quota. The EU's deal with Turkey to block the passage of thousands had thrust the story back into the international headlines.

The colleagues who had traveled with me, two tall young men, had become human jungle gyms for a growing number of children. They each had no less than four small bodies attached somewhere on their arms, legs, or shoulders. There was laughter and mud everywhere. I shivered in my hoodie and pulled my already-wet cap down over my eyes.

Sensing someone was watching me, I looked behind me to see two young girls with intertwined arms. Their hair was trapped under scarves, leaving their faces naked. Their long, dark skirts peeked out from beneath long woolen coats that belted in the middle. I could see them shivering beneath their layers and was surprised they didn't move away when I met their gaze. I began to feel awkward as we stood and stared at one another, so I waved. "Hello?"

5. Office of the United Nations High Commissioner for Refugees.

One of the girls, who wore a sky-blue hijab, responded in heavily accented English. "Hello?"

Her headscarf was distracting— a constant visual reminder of their world, their beliefs, and the threat they posed to my way of life.

Two pairs of expectant eyes still stared, wanting more from me. I sighed. "What are your names?"

"Raha," the girl in blue answered quickly. Her eyes danced and I was surprised to realize that they too were blue.

"I am Eden." I spoke slowly, trying to be clear. "And you," I nodded to the other girl. "What is your name?"

This one was shyer. Her eyes dropped behind long eyelashes. "Namar."

"You are sisters?" I asked.

Two pair of eyes stared back at me. They didn't understand. *Very limited English,* I thought to myself. I looked back to see that my jungle-gym colleagues were still surrounded by their gang of kids.

"Come?" The blue-eyed girl motioned to me.

I scanned the horizon, unsure of what to do. *Was I safe here?* Way down the path, one policeman sat in his blue-and-white compact car.

"Come?" The girl said again. It was still a question, but it had more urgency now. I felt her arm snaking around mine as she gently tugged me forward.

Though I hadn't yet decided whether I should follow, she led me away from the central space and toward the back of the gas station, past an outdoor water faucet built by the anti-trafficking group A21. Women in hijabs, with skirts wrapped around their ankles, crouched at the edge of the mud, stretching their raw hands into the ice-cold water to wring out laundry. I marveled that humanity managed to organize itself into some sort of sense even without the usual structures meant to maintain social order. It was hard to believe that these inhumane conditions existed in Europe.

As we wove around tent posts toward a quieter, inner sanctum of the camp, the landscape changed. *Where am I going?* The words pounded in my head as I realized there were far more men here than there had been at the front of the camp.

These were the military-aged men the media warned about—they were everywhere. *A temporary refugee camp is the conduit to bring terrorists in and spread them across Europe*—the thought made my heart pound as the article took shape in my mind. I wondered how to snap photos without being noticed . . . I was afraid of what would happen if they did notice.

Suddenly, we stopped at the entrance of a large, white tent emblazoned with the letters UNHCR. Raha bent down and called inside. After a moment, a tall man in his mid-thirties stepped out of the tent into the rain, closing the flap behind him. I felt his gaze on me but avoided eye contact as rapid-fired Arabic swirled around me. I grew more nervous as two more young men approached. One had a hoodie pulled over his ears and a red-and-white bandana tied loosely around his neck. Could I wrestle my arm from Raha's grasp and run? What were the chances I could make it back to the entrance, to my colleagues?

"My cousin," the man dug his hands into his pockets and nodded toward Raha, "would like to learn about you, but she does not speak English. I am Zahid. I was an English teacher in Syria. I will translate for you. Will you come in?" Pulling back the flaps of the white UNHCR tent, he invited us to take shelter from the rain.

The interior of the tent was clean, with a few cloth bags—filled with their meager belongings, I assumed—lining the edges. The man's young son and daughter played in the middle of the space as his wife, heavily pregnant, leaned against one of the bags for support. Pausing before the second flap of the tent, I removed my shoes and touched one socked foot to the floor. The cold, muddy water broke the barrier immediately, and I shivered at the unexpected sensation.

"Will you take coffee or tea?" Zahid asked.

I blinked in surprise. Looking around me, I wondered where and how they could produce a hot drink inside the tent. I felt the adrenaline rush beginning to slow as I realized that these people meant me no harm. In fact, they were offering me hospitality.

"I'm fine," I gulped.

"You are my guest. It is the least I can do. Maybe both? The boys will bring it and you can decide." He looked to the two young men who had sparked my fear. They turned and went back into the cold rain.

As our conversation wandered through the basics, we began to get to know one another. His children, a five-year-old girl and six-year-old boy, were sweet. His wife, five months pregnant with their third child, feared she would have to give birth in the tent. Raha and Namar asked questions of their own and patiently waited for Zahid to translate. Their eyes rarely left my face now.

The two young men brought me strong tea that scalded my hands through the thin paper cup, but it warmed my chilled insides. I was feeling bolder now and broached a topic I'd been wondering about. "You know, a lot of people believe you should have stayed in Aleppo to fight against ISIS."

Zahid looked at me, perhaps gauging whether I was one of those people, then said, "Sure, I read the news." He pointed to his old smartphone. "We stayed until they dropped a bomb on our house. It was night and we slept in the basement. If we had been in the top floors . . . " He trailed off, then took a breath. "Nobody got hurt, and we left the next day. Now we are here. How can Europe keep us in this situation?"

"I'm sorry," I said.

He shrugged. "My country was beautiful. We had a good life and I didn't want to leave, but war steals your choices."

An uncomfortable silence stretched between us. I had nothing to say. I wasn't sure if I believed all he had said, and I was ready to leave. It seemed awkward not to offer to help. I had taken photos and conducted an interview. "Is there something you need?" I asked. "Some way I can help? I could . . . I don't know, bring you something next time I come?"

"I appreciate your offer, but we aren't chickens." The clipped reply came quickly. The anger in his voice surprised me. It was the first time in our conversation I had sensed anything other than gracious hospitality.

Noticing my quizzical look, he sighed and explained, "We aren't chickens. You can't just give us a little food and cover our cages with a blanket so we'll be quiet in these inhumane conditions. We are humans, after all." He pointed toward the border with Macedonia that lay just 30 kilometers away. "Can you open that border and let us through?"

"No."

"Then you can't help us," he replied bitterly. He softened his tone. "Thank you for offering. I don't mean to be rude. It's just that we are not poor people. I provided well for my family in Syria. I just need a safe place for them now."

Reflect on this . . .

Take time to think about what you have in common with people from other countries.

Why do we spend so much time focusing on our differences?

In what ways can we find common ground with people who are not like us?

NOTES:

6

Eden Writes

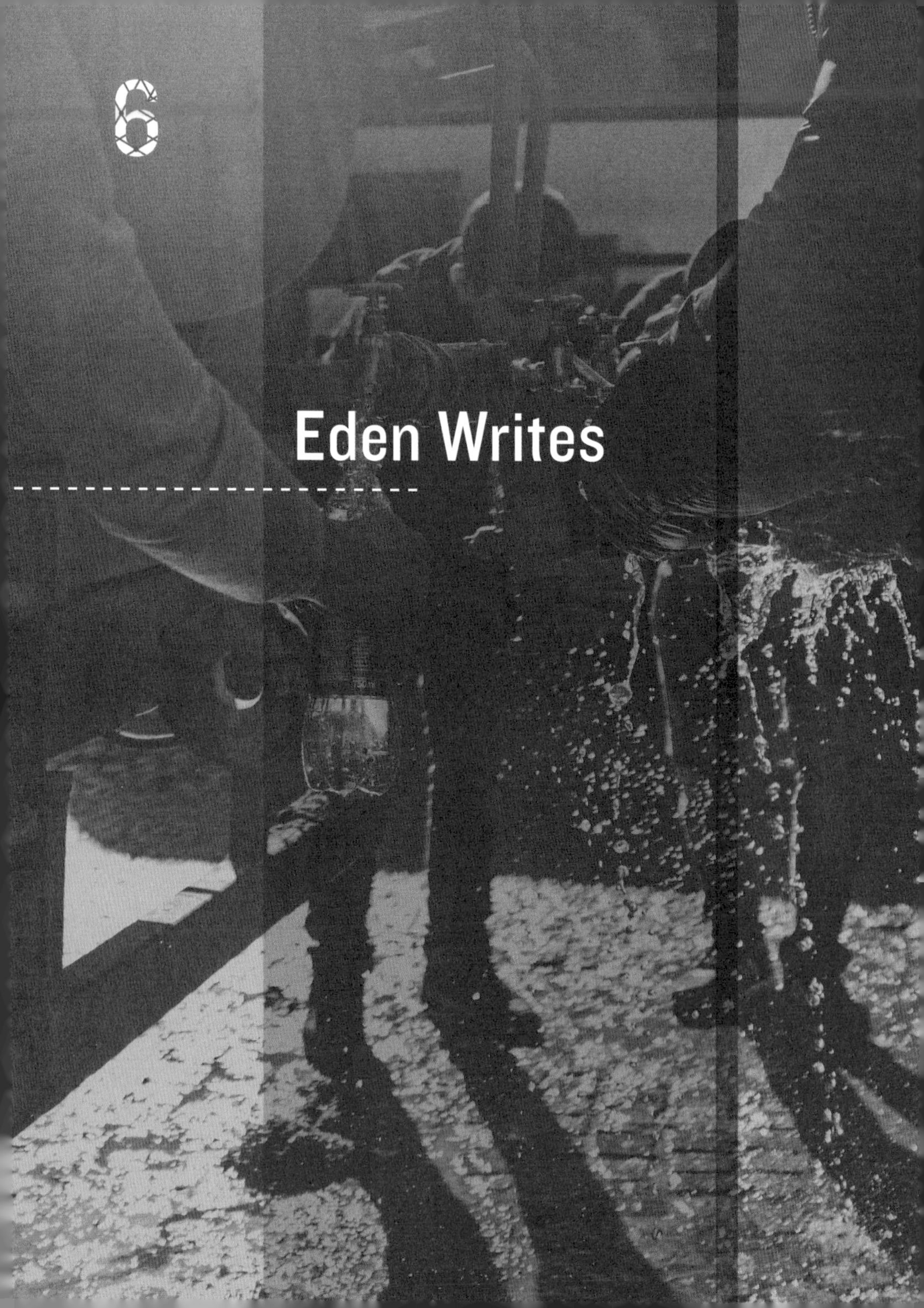

July 2016, in the Central Park of Belgrade, Serbia

By now, reports of police brutality were skyrocketing. While I was interested in that story, I was more interested in the story that would sell—the story of the refugees' illegal activities. Not only were they illegally crossing borders, they were hiring smugglers to help them make their crossings.

"Sophia, Natalya, let's go," I called across the room. "We're gonna be late." They were both still in bed, trying to put off waking up. I heard a sleep-fogged "Coming." Five minutes later, they had slipped into jeans and T-shirts and emerged blurry-eyed from the room.

As we walked from our hostel to the park, I briefed them. "Okay, like I told you, we're joining a group that's distributing water to the refugees in the park. You guys help with that and I'll work on interviewing people, okay?"

"I brought my notebook, Aunt Eden," piped Sophia. "I'll get some interviews too."

"That's fine," I said. "Just remember to stay together. And be careful around these people. Is that clear?"

After a five minute walk, we were entering a smaller piece of the public park connected to the city's main bus and train station. "This is Afghani Park," I explained to the girls. "They call it that because last year, when the first wave of refugees came through, the Afghanis stayed in this part. Water distribution happens over there." I pointed toward the bigger section of park, across the busy street.

We crossed and walked up just as a young blond man was giving instructions. I knew him as Felix, a British national who volunteered as the coordinator for a Serbian NGO[6].

"We have over 1,000 bottles of water that have been donated, and our goal is simply to keep people hydrated in this heat," he told the assembled volunteers. "We'll meet back here in 90 minutes to debrief."

As he finished giving instructions, Sophia and Natalya filled their backpacks with water bottles. "Remember to stay together," I told them. I picked up a few bottles too and walked off to get my interviews.

Amina, Leila, and Omar

Amina fanned her face as she sat on the blanket, loosening the scarf around her neck and cheeks in hopes of catching a rare breeze. She was tired of the heat and the travel. Or maybe she was just tired of being homeless. Not knowing if they would eat or where they would sleep was exhausting.

She looked down at her four-year-old, who was quietly paging through a picture book. She smiled. At least the kids seemed to be doing okay today, though the heat had managed to slow even little Leila down. A thought struck her. *Where is Omar?* It had been over an hour since she'd last seen the boy. She scanned the crowd, straining for a glimpse of his tall, lanky frame.

"Would you like a water?"

Amina jumped and looked up to see two blond girls towering over her. She processed the words for a few moments before replying. "Water . . . ? Yes,

---

6. A non-governmental organization (NGO) is a not-for-profit organization that is independent from states and international governmental organizations.< https://en.wikipedia.org/wiki/Non-governmental_organization> Accessed April 13, 2017.

thank you." The words tumbled haltingly from her mouth. It had been a while since she'd last spoken English.

"Sit down, please." She motioned to a space on her blanket as the taller girl pulled a water from her bag.

"Oh, thanks." The girl bent her long legs into a pretzel shape while taking a long draw of water from her own bottle. "What's your name?"

"My name is Amina. What is your name?"

"I am Natalya. This is Sophia, my sister."

Amina's breath caught in her throat, and she barely managed to hold back her tears. She took a drink of her water, forcing the lump in her throat back down.

Quickly composing herself, she shook the girl's hand. "Natalya. Hello." Turning to the younger sister, she forced the name through her lips. "Sophia. Hello." She pulled two apples from her bag, feeling their weight and coolness in her hand. "I can offer you an apple, if you like." They were the last two she had—last night's thieves had taken the rest, along with their money and their documents.

As Sophia reached for the apple, Natalya's hand shot out to stop her. "It's okay," Amina assured. "She can take it. Please. It makes me happy to give you something. I am sorry I do not have more."

They sat together in a sea of similar blankets and people scattered across the grass. Amina noticed there were other foreigners dotted across the park, also giving water. "You are with these people?" Amina asked.

"Yes, we're giving water," said Natalya. "Later tonight, we'll be back to give food. Do you know where to go to get the food?"

Amina shook her head. The question triggered recollections of all the obstacles they had overcome just to survive this long. Food was always a concern, of course. Leila had a long scrape on her arm where razor wire had torn into it, and Omar had a deep bite from the dogs the guards had loosed on them. *How would we have made this trip with the baby too?* Her thoughts were interrupted by Sophia.

"Where are you from?"

Amina smiled. "Kabul, in Afghanistan. And you?"

Sophia laughed. "Well, that's complicated. In the States for now, I guess." Her brow furrowed. "So why did you leave Kabul?"

"I am a doctor."

"A doctor?" The girls exclaimed in unison.

"Women work in Afghanistan?" Sophia blurted. "I thought—well, you're wearing a scarf, so I thought that meant you're Muslim and you're not allowed to work . . . ?" Her thought trailed into a question.

Amina smiled. "I am a doctor, and I was a teaching professor too. I was training women to be doctors. And yes, I am Muslim. Let me show you a photo of my last group of students." She pulled out her phone, the one thing the thieves had missed the night before. Flipping past photos of her family, holiday celebrations, and her apartment, she stopped at a series of pictures showing a group of eight women posing with her. "This is my last class of doctors. I am sorry to say that the hospital where this was taken has now been destroyed."

"Really?" Natalya settled back onto the blanket. "I thought there was only a war in Syria."

Amina shook her head. "No, we also have fighting. The Taliban has control of some parts of Afghanistan. They are fighting to take Kabul and . . . " A new shadow fell across the blanket. Omar was finally back. Amina breathed a sigh of relief, then said, "Say hello to our guests, Omar. This is Natalya and Sophia."

"Hello," the girls chimed together.

"Sa-a-lam Aley-kum," Omar intoned.

"Try your English," Amina instructed. "You must practice."

Omar glanced at her, then awkwardly said, "Hello. I am Omar. Nice meet you."

"Very good English," laughed Sophia. "Come and practice with us. So, Amina is your mom?"

Amina watched the boy and her heart ached for him.

Slowly, he shook his head. "No. My mother, my father, they are . . ." He paused to search for the right word.

Amina leaned forward and said quietly, "His parents were killed in Kabul. The Taliban. He was traveling alone and we met him in Greece. He is with us now."

"So, you knew him from before?" asked Natalya.

"No," a shadow crossed over her face. "No, we did not know him, but he was alone, with no family. It is dangerous for a 14-year-old boy to travel alone. So now, he is our family."

"Wow," said Sophia. Looking at Omar, she said sincerely, "I'm sorry about your parents."

He would have replied, but a foreign woman had appeared at the edge of the blanket.

Natalya explained, “This is our aunt,” Natalya said. “She’s a journalist.” It was almost imperceptible, but it seemed like the girl had rolled her eyes.

“Good-bye, girls.” Amina smiled. “Thank you for visiting.”

The girls were beginning to stand, when suddenly Sophia reached down to Amina and gave her a spontaneous hug. “It was really nice to meet you,” she said. “You’re a good mother.” Amina’s eyes immediately welled with tears.

The foreign woman snapped her fingers. “Girls, let’s go. I’m in a rush.”

As the girls trailed away, Amina looked back down at her phone, now in Leila’s hands. The little girl was flipping through photos and stopped at one. “Sophia,” she said, pointing at the screen.

Amina suppressed a sob. “Yes. You remember your baby sister?” It was the last photo she had of her six-month-old daughter, taken just a day before she was killed in a Taliban attack. Amina felt her chest ache for the baby she would never hold again, and with Leila and Omar beside her, she let a tear fall.

Karam Hires a Smuggler

Karam lay stretched on his side, resting his head on his palm and kicking the ground with his toe. To those around him, today was a typical day—one more day in an endless string of days with nothing to do, nowhere to go, and nothing ahead but hours of monotony. Waiting, always waiting, always bored.

But for Karam, today was different. Today, he felt a surge of fear rise up in his chest. Anticipation of the dangers that lay ahead of him tonight consumed his thoughts. Even the mind-numbing boredom of the camp offered no reprieve, no escape. He lay there with image after image of what could happen, how it could all go wrong, looping in his mind. He could be caught. He could be killed.

"Hey, Karam," Audi called, breaking into his anxious thoughts. "Football? Come on."

Karam looked over at his friend and tried to ignore the butterflies in his stomach. "Just a few kicks, okay? I got something to do later."

"What are you doing later?" The boy looked at him, his foot resting on the ball.

"Just something."

Audi watched him for a moment. "You're crossing the border tonight." It was a statement, not a question.

Karam looked him in the eye. "Yeah." There was no reason to lie. Everyone here had a smuggler. Some referred to them as "agents," somehow making them sound like travel agents for a holiday trip. But this was no holiday. And travel agents didn't charge $1,500 for illegal midnight border crossings.

A Story with No Ending

I looked at the clock on the nightstand. My deadline was drawing ever-closer. At any other time, I would have been anxious, scrambling, rushing to pound out the story as fast as I could type. Nothing was more important than a deadline.

Or at least, that's what I'd always thought. But right now, all that had been pushed somewhere to the back of my mind by the message I'd just received. It was still there on my phone, haunting me. I was fighting my conscience and regretting getting involved in the first place. *Why had I given Zahid my full name? Why had I friended him on Facebook?* My experiences over the past year had slowly been chipping away at the neat, black-and-white beliefs I had held for so long, and for whatever reason, this one small thing—Zahid's message—had sent it all tumbling down. I didn't know what to believe anymore. But I knew that whatever lay ahead, things had just become more complicated. I picked up the phone to look at the message, and the accompanying photo showing a newborn baby swaddled in homespun rags, once again.

Hi, Eden,

My wife gave birth to a baby girl yesterday. I was happy that an NGO helped us leave the EKO station and go to a hospital. It was hard, but my wife and the baby are okay. We named her "Beautiful Light." We are still waiting to leave this camp to begin a new life with our children.

All the best to you as you write our story.

Zahid

Reflect on this . . .

If you were a refugee, to what lengths would you go to get your family to safety?

How does understanding the issues refugees face help shape your thoughts and feelings toward them?

NOTES:

7

Where They Are Now

As you read each name, think about the thousands of people who have walked the same road that these people have walked . . . and are still walking today.

Bara'ah and baby Zinat: After they crossed the border into Slovenia, they did not continue contact. Their location is unknown.

The newlyweds, Hiba and Muhammed: It is unknown whether they made it to Germany, which was their destination at the time. They joined the march of approximately 1,000 refugees who left Keleti for Vienna on foot.

The mother who gave birth at Röszke: While the birth on the border was documented in newspapers and United Nation reports, the destination of the family is unknown.

Tereza and the Czech Team: Tereza remained active in helping refugees for several months as a volunteer. The Czech Team NGO won recognition for their effective work along the Balkan route.

The mother who fainted at Bobska: Ahmed, the man who cared for her three-year-old son, waited until the mother regained consciousness. Later, a UNHCR volunteer was able to help reunite the eight-year-old girl with her mother and brother after over four hours of waiting in the cold. The whereabouts of Ahmed and the family are unknown.

Maram, her daughter Hasna, and their family of five from Damascus: Their destination is unknown.

Namar, Raha, and their families: Still at the Northern Greek border waiting to be reassigned to a country.

Zahid, his wife, and their three children: After choosing to not use a smuggler, the family waited six months at the Greek border to be reassigned. They are currently temporary residents in another country on the Balkan route. They are housed in a one-room apartment with 100 other refugees. Their status is uncertain. At four months, the baby caught pneumonia and fought for her life.

Amina, Leila, and Omar: After they left the park in Belgrade, Amina made contact with Eden a few times. Eventually, she stopped calling.

Karam: After getting caught attempting to cross the border using a smuggler, Karam was unable to pay another smuggler for a second attempt. He and his mother continue to wait in a camp in Northern Greece. As the school year began, the 14-year-old took to Facebook to lament the fact that he could not go to school. He dreams of being a math teacher one day.

And as for me, Eden? Where am I now?

Somewhere in my year of wandering with refugees, I found my own face tucked behind the hijab and the heart and the hospitality. Encountering the displaced, I came to realize that I am them and they are me. In each face I saw, I saw my own. We are all created in His image; we have all fallen from grace. During my journey, I found the piece of my humanity that wrestles with the sinfulness of who I became in the Garden—separated from God by my choice to look inward, rather than upward. Yet, the promise of the God-man—He who would give me safe passage across the borders of earth and eternity— stands at my door. He knocks. He waits.

I am troubled, tossed about in an ocean of change—a tidal wave of politics and controversy. All the while, I am searching, constantly searching, for a refuge where my faith can walk on water. I wonder—at the beginning of time, when God created the oceans, did He have my fear in mind? Did He know how it would swell deep inside me?

I wrote my story in finger-taps on a keyboard. I captured the faces of humanity with the click of my camera and carried them all on my back across kilometers and cultures. I put them together to tell the story that was being born in my heart: The story that shouts of fear, moans with prejudice, and whispers grace in the ebb and the flow of this journey from Greece to Hungary to Serbia to Croatia, and beyond.

I hope you hear their voices too—the displaced voices that are tangled and woven in the midst of mine. I hope you hear my pain, confusion, and fear. But please, don't let my voice drown out the thunder of a million feet—the sound of those who ran from the terror of war to face their own fears upon raging waters and foreign lands.

Fear, I have found, is no respecter of persons or culture or language or religion. Fear is a force. Yet, in the face of perfect love, and only perfect love, it finds its defeat. God's love has the power to cast out fear and fill our lives with His presence.

I hope you find the cadence of my words different here in this last chapter. For it is from this place that I stand and peer backwards, past the last two years and across the spans of time to a small place in Bethlehem, where Rachel's mourning voice sends a Nazarene family into exile in Egypt. From that place, a baby King emerges wearing the crown of "refugee." He journeys to the cross and breaks the walls that divide us with the name *Yeshua*—God with us.

You'll find me here on the journey with the other wanderers from far-off lands. Our human struggle, our search for sanctuary, and our eternal destiny are defined by the borders of a garden in Genesis and the promise of a new heaven and earth. We are all traveling a path toward home. We are all walking in a strange land. *We all share the name refugee.*

With courage,

Eden Walker ●

Reflect on this...

In what ways has this book changed your concept of a refugee?

What are the ways you can reach out to the refugees in your community, state, country, and world?

What has God shown you through the stories told in this book?

NOTES:

Other Dialog studies also available!

HOLY LIVING

What It Means to Be like Christ

God has commanded us in His Word that we are to be "holy as He is holy." But is this really possible? What does it mean to live a holy life? Is holiness only reasonable for those who have it all together or never make a mistake?

PARTICIPANT'S GUIDE ISBN: 978-0-8341- 3432-4
FACILITATOR'S GUIDE ISBN: 978-0-8341-3431-7

PRESSURE POINTS

Practical Faith for Facing Life's Challenges

Every life has its share of ups and downs. Often when we express our thoughts, feelings, and questions to others, we get helpful advice that only seems to scratch the surface of our searching hearts. Pressure Points: Practical Faith for Facing Life's Challenges digs deep into areas of life that have a profound impact on us and examines practical ways we can face each challenge successfully.

PARTICIPANT'S GUIDE ISBN: 978-0-8341- 3536-9
FACILITATOR'S GUIDE ISBN: 978-0-8341-3535-2

Available online at DialogSeries.com